FAR OUT

How to Create Your Own Star World

FAR OUT

How to Create Your Own Star World

by Robin West

photographs by Bob and Diane Wolfe

drawings by Priscilla Kiedrowski

 Carolrhoda Books, Inc./Minneapolis

to Paul H. Engfer

This book is available in two editions:
Library binding by Carolrhoda Books, Inc.
Soft cover by First Avenue Editions
241 First Avenue North
Minneapolis, Minnesota 55401

Library of Congress Cataloging-in-Publication Data

West, Robin.
  Far out!

  Summary: Instructions for using household materials to make such star world items as an astro shuttle, a meteor man, and a lunar colony computer.
    1. Outer space—Exploration—Juvenile literature.
2. Space vehicles—Models—Juvenile literature.
[1. Outer space—Exploration. 2. Space vehicles—
Models. 3. Handicraft] I. Wolfe, Robert L., ill.
II. Wolfe, Diane, ill. III. Kiedrowski, Priscilla, ill.
IV. Title.
TL793.W47 1987   629.4′0228   86-16697
ISBN 0-87614-279-X (lib. bdg.)
ISBN 0-87614-463-6 (pbk.)

 2 3 4 5 6 7 8 9 10 97 96 95 94 93 92 91 90 89 88

Contents

Dear Reader,

This book shows you how to make your own star world from materials as down-to-earth as construction paper and as close as your own home or the nearest variety store. Better yet, your star world will work! The Hot Rod Transporter will zoom along the planet's surface, the Astro Shuttle will fly through space, and the Interplanetary Rover will roam the land.

The directions are easy to follow. I've divided each project into three parts. First, I show you how to make the basic form, then I tell you how I decorated mine, and, last, I give you some suggestions to start your own imagination working.

Because the projects in this book take you to outer space, the most important thing you'll need is a free-wheeling, ready-to-go mind. You can copy my ideas on decorating or come up with your own brand-new ones—whatever you want to do. Remember, there are no right answers to decorating when you're in another world, so let your imagination go!

When you've decided what you want to make, read all the instructions carefully before you begin. Then gather all the materials you'll need. You'll probably want to work on old newspapers so that spilled glue or paint won't matter. Be sure to ask for help if you need it, but, most important, have fun making and playing with your *far out* star world!

Your Basic Equipment

colored construction paper
pencil
ruler
scissors
white liquid glue
Elmer's glue is fine.
clear-drying glue
This can be found in hobby or fabric stores. Ask for Super Tacky glue.
masking tape
poster paints and brushes
colored felt-tip markers
paper punch
This is helpful, but not absolutely necessary.

Things to Save

cans
Tuna fish, soup, and juice cans can be used for tracing circles. Make sure all the cans you are going to use are clean.
string
yarn
plastic straws
cardboard
pipe cleaners
toilet paper tubes

cardboard boxes
These are handy for spray painting. They keep paint spatters and "fog" off of you *and* the room you're working in.

large and small thread spools

large, medium, and small paper or plastic drinking cups

Equipment You Will Need for Only a Few Projects

a few small- and medium-sized nails

straight non-clip clothespins

Ping-Pong balls

egg-shaped panty hose containers

Styrofoam balls in various sizes

sequins

spray paint

wheat paste
This is wallpaper paste.

clear acrylic spray

plastic containers with lids
Look for the ones that dairy toppings and margarine come in.

egg cartons

plastic grid fruit containers

newspapers

tagboard
This is heavy-duty cardboard.

kitchen bowls

dowel sticks
These can be bought at most hobby or dime stores.

cotton swab containers
Find the sliding boxes.

Hot Rod Transporter

Imagine yourself zooming along the surface of a strange planet, transporting special materials and space equipment. In your Hot Rod Transporter with its secret compartment you can break the speed of sound!

You Will Need:

colored construction paper
pencil
ruler
scissors
white liquid glue
masking tape
poster paint and brush
These are optional.
colored felt-tip markers
1 cotton swab sliding box
2 plastic straws
2 pipe cleaners
4 small thread spools

Let's Begin:

1. To achieve a finished exterior for the hot rod body, cover the cotton swab box with colored construction paper and glue it in place as I have or paint it with poster paint. If you use paint, let it dry before you continue.
2. Measure and cut two straws the width of the box body.
3. Tape a straw to each underside end of the body with masking tape.

9

4. Slide a pipe cleaner through each straw.
5. Slide a small thread spool onto each straw end and bend the pipe cleaner ends to secure the spools. Trim the pipe cleaner ends with scissors. You have made the body and wheels of the hot rod.

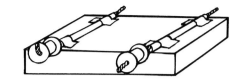

6. To make the handle for the secret sliding compartment at the front of the hot rod, draw and cut a piece of paper ½ inch wide by 4 inches long.
7. Measure 1 inch from each end, then mark and fold along the marks toward the center of the strip.

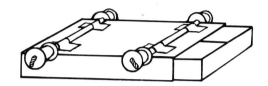

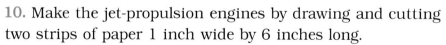

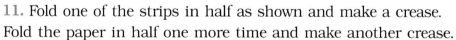

8. Overlap the ends and glue them together.
9. Glue the flat side of the handle to the front of the hot rod secret compartment.

10. Make the jet-propulsion engines by drawing and cutting two strips of paper 1 inch wide by 6 inches long.
11. Fold one of the strips in half as shown and make a crease. Fold the paper in half one more time and make another crease.
12. Open the strip and shape it into a triangle, overlapping the two ends. Glue the ends together.

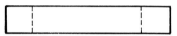

13. Repeat Steps 11 and 12 with the other strip.
14. Glue both triangles side by side to the top end of the back of the hot rod.
15. Make the side wings by drawing and cutting one strip of paper 2 inches wide by 6 inches long.

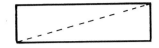

16. Using your ruler, draw a diagonal line corner to corner.
17. Cut along the line to make two wings.
18. Glue one wing to each side of the hot rod.

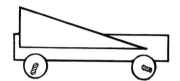

How I Decorated:

Because the Hot Rod Transporter is *so* fast, I cut lightning-bolt flames for the sides of the vehicle. I used paper strips to decorate the jet-propulsion system. I also cut different shapes and designs to decorate the transporter's surface.

More Ideas:

Give your vehicle identification numbers or letters. Use felt-tip markers as well as construction paper or poster paint to decorate.

Astro Shuttle

The Astro Shuttle is the latest in outer-space commuter transportation. You can meet many interesting characters if you buy a ticket and hop on. Don't miss the ride of your life!

You Will Need:

colored construction paper
pencil
ruler
scissors
white liquid glue
poster paints and brushes
These are optional.
colored felt-tip markers
1 quart milk container
string
1 large thread spool
1 medium paper cup

Let's Begin:

1. Cut along the top and bottom edges of one side of the milk carton as shown.
2. On the same side, cut down the center from top to bottom and fold the sides out to form the shuttle wings.

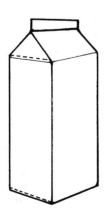 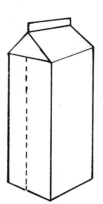 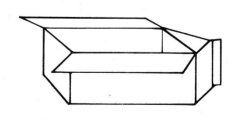

3. Now you can cover the outer body of the shuttle with colored paper or paint it to give it a finished look. If you use paint, let it dry before you continue.

4. Using your scissors point, carefully poke a small hole in each side corner of the shuttle body. (A small nail will also work.)
5. Cut two pieces of string, each 16 inches long.
6. Tie one string end to each corner of the shuttle in the front and knot securely.

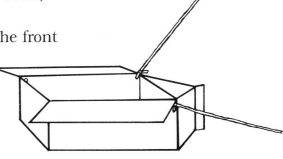

7. Take the large thread spool and slip both strings through the spool hole. Tie one loose thread end to each of the remaining corner holes.

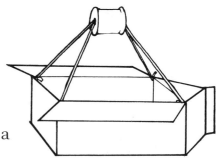

8. The tail of the shuttle is made by cutting off the top of a medium cup.
9. Glue the bottom of the shortened cup to the tail end of the shuttle.

10. To fly the shuttle, slide a long piece of string through the thread spool hole. Attach one end of the string to a chair and the other end to a lower point across the room. The shuttle will zoom across the room and land!

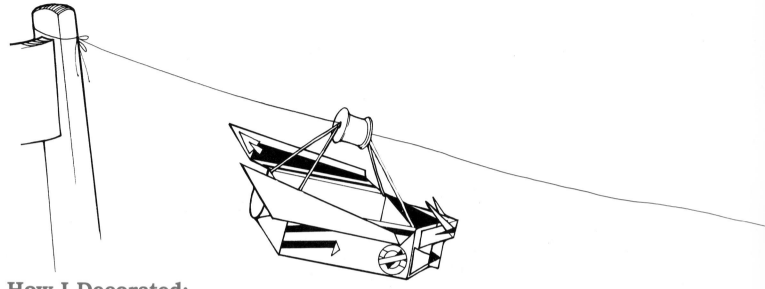

How I Decorated:

I added paper strips to the tail to give it a streamlined rocket appearance. I glued long, skinny triangles to the wings to make them more aerodynamic. You can do the same by drawing and cutting a strip of paper 2 inches wide by 8 inches long. Cut corner to corner and glue one to each wing.

More Ideas:

Add numbers and letters to identify the shuttle. Cut different shapes from colored construction paper to create "alien" emblems and symbols. Use your imagination to come up with ideas for giving the shuttle a "supersonic" look.

Meteor Man

Meteor Man is the friendliest of space beings. At a moment's notice, he will jump into his Astro Shuttle and visit the far corners of space.

You Will Need:

scissors
3 Styrofoam balls, 1½ inches
    diameter
10 Styrofoam balls, 1 inch
    diameter
cardboard box
spray paint
1 nail at least 1½ inches long
6 pipe cleaners
The following items are optional:
colored construction paper
white liquid glue
colored felt-tip markers
sequins

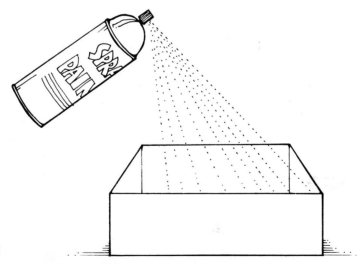

Let's Begin:

1. Place the Styrofoam balls in the cardboard box and spray them with your favorite color of paint. The box will control the rolling balls and trap the paint spray. Allow to dry.

2. Using the nail, carefully punch a hole all the way through the center of each small ball and two of the large balls. Punch a hole halfway through the center of the remaining large ball.

3. Take the half-punched large ball and force a pipe cleaner into the hole for Meteor Man's head.

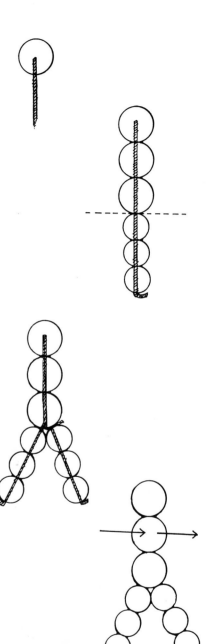

4. Push the remaining two large balls onto the same pipe cleaner to form the trunk of the body.

5. Push three small balls onto the remainder of the pipe cleaner to form one of the legs. Bend the end of the pipe cleaner to secure all the balls and trim with scissors.

6. Take another pipe cleaner and push three balls onto it, bending the end to secure the balls.

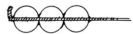

7. Wind the remaining end to the bottom trunk leg connection to form the other leg. You now have the head, trunk, and legs of Meteor Man.

8. To make the arms, slide two small balls onto another pipe cleaner. Bend one end to secure the balls.

9. Using the nail again, poke a hole all the way through the middle large ball of the body as shown.

10. Slide the pipe cleaner with two balls through this hole.
11. Push the two remaining small balls onto the pipe cleaner to form the other arm. Bend to secure the balls and trim.

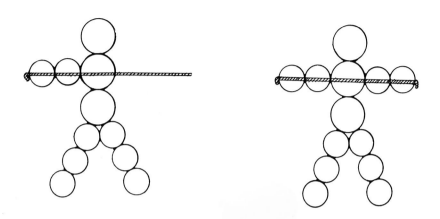

How I Decorated:

I made communication antennae by cutting two small pipe cleaners, gluing sequins to their ends, and sticking them into Meteor Man's head. I cut out white paper eyes and drew round pupils with a felt-tip marker. I also gave Meteor Man a big, paper smile. After all, he is very friendly.

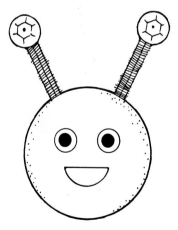

More Ideas:

When you decorate your Meteor Man, use your own idea of how a friendly space being should look. Maybe he has an extra head or only one eye. Anything goes in outer space!

pencil
ruler
2 pipe cleaners, 11 inches long
1 piece of pipe cleaner,
   4 inches long

Meteor Man's
Life-Support Stand

When Meteor Man isn't flying through space, he needs to fuel
up at his life-support stand.

Let's Begin:

1. Measure and mark 3 inches from the end of one of the longer pipe cleaners. Bend at a 90 degree angle as shown.
2. Measure and mark 3 inches in from the first bend. Bend again at a 90 degree angle as shown.

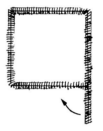

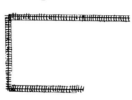

3. Measure and mark 3 inches in from the second bend. Bend one more time at a 90 degree angle as shown.
4. To finish the square, take the short piece of pipe cleaner in the middle and attach one end to the left-over end of the first pipe cleaner by twisting the ends together.
5. Secure the square by bending the short pipe cleaner and twisting the two remaining ends together.
6. Using the remaining pipe cleaner, bend and secure one end to corner Number 1 of the square.
7. Bend and secure the other end of this pipe cleaner to corner Number 2.
8. Bend in the middle as shown. Meteor Man's feet will fit inside the square, and his trunk will rest against the back of the stand.

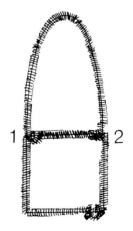

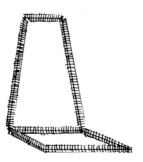

Triangle Transistor

Triangle Transistor is a crazy creature with three-dimensional triangles making up his body, arms, and legs. You will frequently see him with Meteor Man, flying through the heavens and exploring uncharted stars.

You Will Need:

colored construction paper
pencil
ruler
scissors
white liquid glue
clear-drying glue
colored felt-tip markers
These are optional.
1 Ping-Pong ball
1 straight non-clip clothespin
1 soup can
1 small piece of pipe cleaner

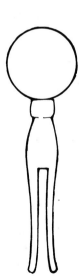

Let's Begin:

1. Glue the Ping-Pong ball to the top of the clothespin with clear-drying glue. Allow to dry.

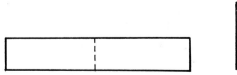
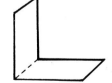

2. Measure and mark, then cut three strips of paper 1 inch wide by 6 inches long.

3. Take one strip and fold it in half as shown. Make a crease.

4. Fold the strip in half one more time and make another crease.

5. Open the strip and shape it into a triangle by overlapping the two ends. Glue these ends together with white liquid glue.

6. Follow Steps 3-5 to form triangles from the other two strips of paper.

7. Glue one of the triangles onto the clothespin below the Ping-Pong ball head as shown. Allow to dry.

8. Glue the other two triangles to one side of the first triangle on each side of the clothespin as shown.

9. To form the legs, draw and cut two strips of paper 2 inches wide by 4 inches long.

10. Follow Steps 3-5 to make two long, skinny triangles.

11. Put glue on the inside of the clothespin leg. Slide one of the triangles up the inside of the leg as shown. Allow to dry.

 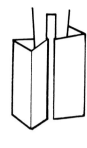

12. Repeat Step 11 with the other triangle.

13. Draw and cut two strips of paper 1¼ inches wide by 4 inches long.

14. Follow Steps 3-5 to make two triangles.

15. Glue each triangle to a front leg triangle as shown.

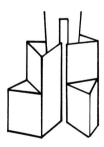

16. Draw and cut two strips of paper ¾ inch wide by 4 inches long.

17. Follow Steps 3-5 to make the last two triangles.

18. Form the feet by gluing these two small triangles to the front legs as shown.

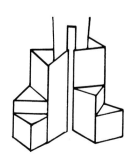

Triangle Transistor's Hat

1. To make the hat, trace around a soup can on a piece of construction paper. Cut out the circle.
2. Find the center of the circle by measuring it from edge to edge. Make a dot at the point half the distance of the total length.

3. From the outer edge of the circle, cut a straight line to the center dot and stop.
4. Overlap the two cut edges and glue to form a cone.
5. Glue this cone onto the Ping-Pong ball head.

How I Decorated:

I repeated Steps 1-4 for the hat, using a smaller circle to make another cone for the transistor antenna. I glued it to a small, bent pipe cleaner—for good reception. Triangle Transistor's face is a combination of paper circles, triangles, rectangles, and stripes glued together in a crazy pattern. Paper lightning bolts, stripes, and circles decorate the body of this special outer-space creature.

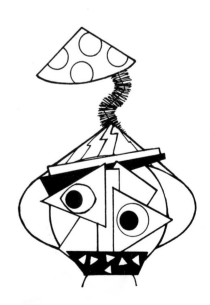

More Ideas:

Give your Triangle Transistor a personal touch by combining the three-dimensional cones you have learned to make with other shapes and designs. Remember, simple shapes can be put together to form spectacular designs!

You Will Need:

colored construction paper
pencil
ruler
scissors
white liquid glue
masking tape
colored felt-tip markers
1 egg-shaped panty hose
  container

Lunar Colony Computer

Every advanced space society has its own computer system, and Lunar Colony is no exception. It possesses a very rare portable computer with a secret interior. You can see it being moved throughout the colony on the Hot Rod Transporter. Don't get too close, though. It might grab you with its accordian arms and never let go!

Let's Begin:

The computer is made by forming a three-dimensional box called a cube.

1. Draw and cut a paper square 3½ inches wide by 3½ inches long. It will be used as a tracing pattern.

2. Using a piece of paper at least 12 inches wide by 18 inches long, trace around the square six times to form a cross shape as shown.

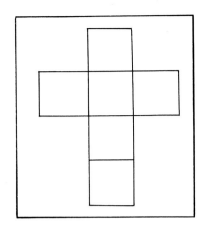

3. Using a ruler, draw lines around the edges of the cross shape as shown by the dotted lines. Cut along these dotted lines.

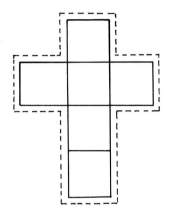

4. Make small diagonal cuts in from the outer edges as shown. Throw away the bits of paper you cut off. You are cutting out tabs that will enable you to fold and glue the cube together.

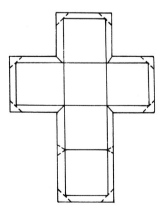

5. Cut off Tabs 4, 5, 8, 9, and 14 as shown to form the shape in the bottom figure.

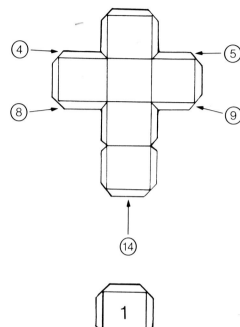

6. Fold on all lines in the same direction—either all up or all under—and carefully make creases.

7. Bring Squares 1, 3, 5, and 6 together to form the sides of the cube.

8. Fold Squares 2 and 4 into place to close the cube and glue carefully. Allow to dry. You have formed the cube.

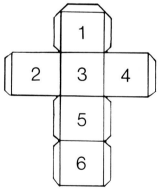

9. To make the computer's arms, draw and cut four strips of paper 1 inch wide by 18 inches long. (*Hint: Your ruler is about 1 inch wide. Line it up against the edge of your paper and draw strips.) You will need two strips to make each arm.

10. Leave 1 inch at one end of the strip for a tab. Glue another strip across the first strip to form an L as shown.
11. Fold Strip 1 over Strip 2 and make a crease.
12. Then fold Strip 2 over Strip 1 and make another crease.
13. Continue Steps 11 and 12 until you run out of paper. You will have many folds and creases.

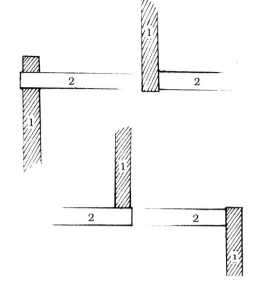

14. Glue the ends together and trim excess paper.
15. Make one more accordian arm with the other two strips by following Steps 10-14.

16. Glue the tabs at the ends of the arms to the side of the cube as shown.

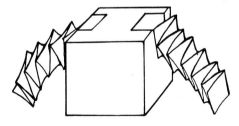

17. Take half of the egg-shaped panty hose container and place masking tape on the inside, extending the tape beyond the edges.

18. Fold the tape so that when you place the egg on top of the computer cube, the tape sticks to the cube top.

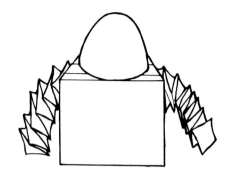

How I Decorated:

I made a secret door by drawing a square on the front of the computer cube. I carefully cut out the top, bottom, and right-hand side of the square door and folded the remaining side.

I also cut three strips of paper and bent and glued their ends to the top of the computer, one on each side and one over the top of the egg. I made two small, three-dimensional triangles and glued them to the egg top for eyes. After all, even a Lunar Colony Computer likes to be able to see.

The grasping, clawlike hands were made by drawing and cutting a square 2 inches wide by 2 inches long. I found the center of the square by measuring it from edge to edge. I made a dot at the point half the distance of the total length. I cut in from one corner to the center dot and stopped. By over-lapping the cut edges and gluing them together, I made it look three-dimensional instead of flat. Finally, I cut out tiny, white triangles and glued these "claws" to the ends of the hands.

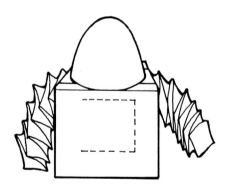

Odd-shaped bits of paper were added to give the computer a colorful, complicated look.

More Ideas:

Think of other ways to decorate the surface of your computer. You could paint or use felt-tip markers to add symbols, emblems, and other computer-type markings.

Cosmic Centipede

The Cosmic Centipede doesn't know which way she is going. She has a head on both ends of her colorful body! Once she does decide her direction of travel, her many legs get her over rough terrain in record time.

You Will Need:

colored construction paper
pencil
ruler
scissors
white liquid glue
poster paint and brush
This is optional.
colored felt-tip markers
These are optional.
1 toilet paper tube
1 small nail at least 2 inches long
3 pipe cleaners

Let's Begin:

1. Cosmic Centipede's body is made by covering a toilet paper tube with construction paper, as I did, or by painting the tube with poster paint. If you use paint, let it dry before going on.

2. Measure and mark three dots at 1 inch, 2½ inches, and 4 inches from one end of the tube as shown.

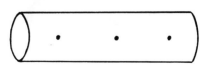

3. Using the nail, puncture a hole at each dot, continuing through the other side of the tube.

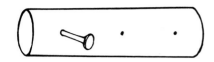

4. Slide a pipe cleaner all the way through each set of holes. Bend the pipe cleaners to form the legs as shown.

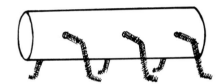

5. Draw and cut one strip of paper 1¼ inches wide by 6 inches long.
6. Fold the strip in half and make a crease.

7. Then fold the strip in half one more time and make another crease.

8. Open the strip and shape it into a triangle by overlapping the two ends. Glue the ends together.

9. Draw and cut another strip of paper ½ inch wide by 4 inches long.

10. Follow Steps 6-8 to form another, smaller triangle. Each triangle serves as a head for Cosmic Centipede.

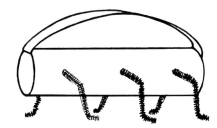

11. To make the bumpy back, draw and cut one strip of paper ½ inch wide by 10 inches long.

12. Glue one end of the strip to the top of the tube at one end.

13. Glue the remaining end to the opposite end of the tube.

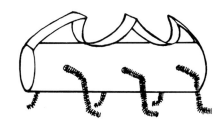

14. Bend and fold this strip at selected points along the back of the tube to give it an accordian look.

15. Glue the two triangles from Steps 5-10 along the back strip, one at the front and the other at the back.

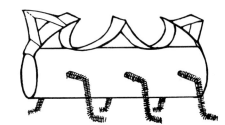

How I Decorated:

Using bits of colored paper and pipe cleaner pieces, I glued a variety of shapes on different parts of the body to make Cosmic Centipede colorful.

More Ideas:

Make more three-dimensional triangles or use felt-tip markers to decorate the body. Add extra legs, eyes, arms--whatever you can imagine!

Solar Saucer

This solar-powered saucer is flown by the Saucerettes and features a moveable ramp for boarding and departing ease.

Let's Begin:

1. Cut a hole next to the edge of the large plastic lid for the ramp opening. Be careful when cutting the plastic. You might need help. The hole should be big enough to drop a Ping-Pong ball through.

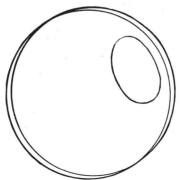

You Will Need:

colored construction paper
pencil
ruler
scissors
white liquid glue
clear-drying glue
colored felt-tip markers
These are optional.
1 large plastic lid
This should be the size of a dairy topping container lid.
1 small plastic lid
This should be the size of a margarine container lid.
1 large plastic or paper drinking cup
1 medium plastic or paper drinking cup
1 Ping-Pong ball
1 toilet paper tube

2. Turn the large drinking cup upside down and apply clear-drying glue around the bottom as shown.

3. Making sure the edge of the large lid is up, center the lid on the cup bottom and press down lightly. Allow to dry.

4. To make the sides of the saucer, cut a strip of paper 2 inches wide by 22 inches long. If you don't have paper long enough, cut two strips 2 inches wide by 12 inches long and glue the ends together.

5. Glue the ends of the long strip together to form a circle the size of the interior edge of the large lid.

6. Place the circle strip onto the top of the large lid. You can either leave it free, as I did, or glue it down.

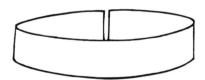

7. Turn the medium cup upside down and apply clear-drying glue to the bottom.

8. Center the small lid, edge side up, on the medium cup bottom and press down lightly. Allow to dry. You have made the base for the upper portion of the saucer.

9. Cut twelve strips of paper ½ inch wide by 6 inches long.
10. Space and glue them to the underside of the small lid. Fold downward so that they hang correctly.

11. To make the ramp for the saucer, cut the toilet paper tube in half lengthwise.

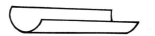

12. At one end of the half-tube, make two small cuts and fold the flap back. The folded sections will anchor the ramp to the saucer floor when in use by the Saucerettes. It can be stored inside the saucer when not in use.

How I Decorated:

I cut flame shapes and glued them to the saucer base. Blast off! I added solar panels and windows to the sides of the saucer body. I cut strips of paper and bent them at the top of the saucer body to form an observation dome. Finally, I added paper circles, squares, and triangles to decorate.

More Ideas:

Add numbers or letters to identify your saucer. Use felt-tip markers and other materials to decorate. Add details that will make your saucer appear to spin in space.

You Will Need:

colored construction paper
pencil
scissors
clear-drying glue
colored felt-tip markers
Ping-Pong balls
You'll need one for each Saucerette.

cardboard box
spray paint
sequins

Saucerettes

The Solar Saucer is their home; about the universe they roam.

Let's Begin:

1. Place the Ping-Pong balls in the cardboard box and spray them with your favorite paint color. The box will control the rolling balls and trap the paint spray. Allow to dry.

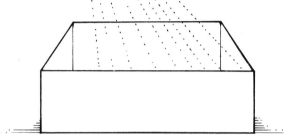

2. To make the base for each Saucerette, draw and cut a strip of paper ¼ inch wide by 4 inches long.
3. Glue the ends together to form a circle. This base will keep your Saucerette from rolling away.

How I Decorated:

I used different-sized sequins to make the eyes and mouths, and I used stars for the noses. Then I glued them to each Saucerette. I cut more sequins in half and glued them both separately and on top of one another to create crazy effects.

More Ideas:

However you choose to decorate the surface, it must remain flat so that the Saucerettes can roll around when not on their bases. Use colored felt-tip markers or construction paper as well as sequins. Make hair from pieces of string or yarn or draw eyelashes and other features.

colored construction paper
pencil
ruler
scissors
white liquid glue
masking tape
colored felt-tip markers
These are optional.
egg-shaped panty hose
  containers
You'll need one for each creature.

Orbital Be-Bops

You can't mistake the Orbital Be-Bops—they are definitely
from outer space. They travel near and far in the Interplanetary Rover with the Saucerettes as their guides—a
far-out combination of friends!

Let's Begin:

1. Draw and cut a strip of paper 1 inch wide by 10 inches long.
2. Bend this strip into a circle and glue the ends together. This is the base.

3. To attach the base to the egg-shaped container, cut three pieces of masking tape and attach them to the inside of the base as shown.

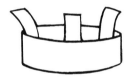

4. Place the base against the more rounded end of the egg and press the masking tape down onto the egg.

How I Decorated:

As you can see, the Orbital Be-Bops can be decorated in many ways. I have used paper rectangles, triangles, and circles. I have also cut out crazy shapes and put them together to form colorful, interesting eyes, noses, mouths, ears, wings, and so on.

More Ideas:

Think about combining some of the shapes, three-dimensional and flat, that you have learned to make in other projects. Give one of the Be-Bops accordian arms or a cone-shaped hat. Use your wildest imagination.

You Will Need:

colored construction paper
pencil
ruler
scissors
white liquid glue
clear-drying glue
colored felt-tip markers
2 Ping-Pong balls
yarn scraps

Bleep and Peep

Bleep and Peep are silly looking, but looks can be deceiving. Each has an advanced intellect that aids them in flying the Supersonic Space Patroller throughout the universe.

Let's Begin:

1. Cut a strip of construction paper 1 inch wide by 4 inches long.
2. Glue the ends of the strip together to form a circular tube shape.

3. Apply clear-drying glue to the top edge.
4. Set the ball on top of the glued edge and allow to dry. You have made the basic body.
5. Follow Steps 1-4 to make a second body.

How I Decorated:

I gave Bleep and Peep hair by gluing bits of yarn to their heads. I also cut shapes to give their faces an "out-of-this-world" appearance.

More Ideas:

Give Bleep and Peep interesting facial and body features by using colored felt-tip markers. Glue sequins to their bases. Use different-colored Ping-Pong balls or paint them with poster paint before you make their bodies. Remember, this *is* outer space.

Interplanetary Rover

Go mobile in this land rover. Bleep and Peep do the driving, so you can sit back and enjoy the scenery.

You Will Need:

colored construction paper
pencil
ruler
scissors
white liquid glue
clear-drying glue
colored felt-tip markers
2 plastic grid fruit containers
string or yarn
4 Styrofoam balls, 2 inches
   diameter
2 dowel sticks, ¼ inch
   diameter by 6½ inches long
2 plastic straws

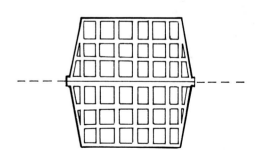

Let's Begin:

1. Put one fruit container on top of the other.
2. With small pieces of string, tie the top to the bottom at the corners of one side only.

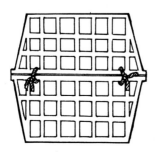

3. To make the wheel assemblies, punch a hole halfway into each of the four Styrofoam balls with a dowel stick.
4. Fill the holes of two of the balls with clear-drying glue.
5. Push a separate dowel stick into each of the two, glue-filled holes. Allow to dry.
6. Cut the two straws into pieces 4 inches long.
7. Slide each straw through the sides of the vehicle as shown.
8. Secure the straws by tying them to the plastic grids with string or yarn.

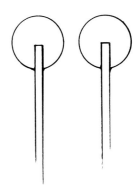

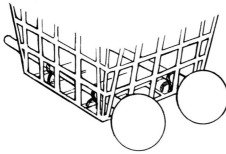

9. Slide the stick-and-ball assemblage made in Steps 3-5 into each straw.
10. Fill the holes of the two remaining Styrofoam balls with clear-drying glue and slide them onto the remaining stick ends. Allow to dry.

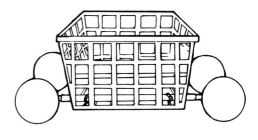

Outside Seating

1. To make outside seating for the space creatures such as Bleep and Peep, draw and cut two squares of paper 3 inches wide by 3 inches long.
2. Find the center of one of the squares by measuring it from edge to edge. Make a dot at the halfway point.
3. From a corner of the square, cut to the dot and stop.

4. To form the triangular seat, overlap the two cut edges to form a point and glue together.

5. Repeat Steps 2-4 to make the other seat.

6. Punch two holes on one edge of each seat.

7. Slide string or yarn through the holes and tie to the top plastic grids of the Interplanetary Rover.

8. To keep Bleep and Peep in their seats during high-speed travel, draw and cut two strips of paper 1 inch wide by 2 inches long.

9. Fold the strip in half the long way. Unfold the strip.

10. Fold the strip in half the short way. Unfold the strip.

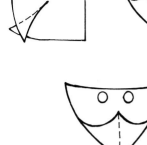

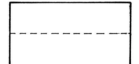
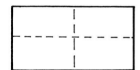
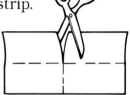

11. On the short center crease, cut from the edge and stop at the crease of the long fold.

12. Fold the short way again to form an angle as shown. Glue the edges that overlap in the middle.

13. Glue to the outer edge of the chair as shown in the photo on page 48.

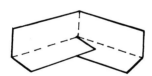

How I Decorated:

On the Interplanetary Rover, I added headlights that appear to be eyes. I also used a bent pipe cleaner as a handle to lift the lid so that passengers can hop inside.

More Ideas:

Weave narrow paper strips in and out of the plastic grids. Give your Rover your own personal touch.

Orbital Ray Detector

Secret messages fly through space! Turn on the Orbital Ray Detector and listen in.

You Will Need:

colored construction paper
pencil
ruler
scissors
white liquid glue
colored felt-tip markers
medium-sized kitchen bowl
A bowl 7-8 inches in diameter is fine.

1 medium paper or plastic cup
1 large thread spool
1 pipe cleaner
paper punch
This is optional.

Let's Begin:

1. To make the detector "ear," draw a circle by tracing around the lip of the bowl. Cut the circle out.

2. Find the center of the circle by measuring it from edge to edge. Make a dot at the halfway point.

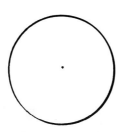

3. From the outer edge of the circle, make a straight cut to the center dot and stop.

4. Form a cone shape by overlapping the edges and gluing them together. Allow to dry.

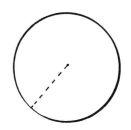

5. Turn the cup upside down and place glue in a straight line across the bottom of the cup as shown.

6. Place the cone shape along the glue line and allow to dry.

7. The power pack is made by putting glue around the outer edge of the thread spool and gluing it into the center of the cone.

 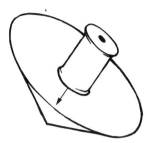 

8. Bend the pipe cleaner in half and force it down the center of the spool hole.

How I Decorated:

I used various-sized paper circles to decorate the Orbital Ray Detector. I added a large circle to the bottom base and smaller ones inside the cone shape. I went crazy with the paper punch and glued small circles everywhere! I covered the spool sides with colored paper and used paper strips to decorate the base.

More Ideas:

Use sequins to give your Detector glitter and shine.

Cosmic Ray Bombarder

A friend and protector to all the Lunar Colony, the Ray Bombarder looks fierce. His arms are a deflecting shield and a powerful cosmic bolt!

You Will Need:

colored construction paper
pencil
ruler
scissors
white liquid glue
masking tape
colored felt-tip markers
scrap of tagboard
This is heavy-duty cardboard.
1 plastic straw
2 pipe cleaners
3 small thread spools

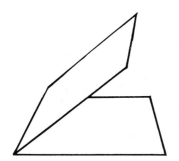

Let's Begin:

1. Draw and cut a strip of paper 3 inches wide by 10 inches long.
2. Fold the strip in half and open it.

3. Measure and mark 2 inches from each end.

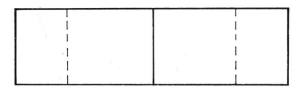

4. Fold these ends toward the center.

5. Bring the ends together and overlap to form a triangle. Glue together.

6. From the tagboard scrap, cut a rectangle 3 inches wide by 2 inches long.
7. Glue this rectangle to the bottom of the three-dimensional triangle to reinforce it. You now have the body.

8. Cut a 5-inch piece of plastic straw.
9. Slide a pipe cleaner through the straw with the ends extended.
10. Slide a thread spool onto each end of the straw. Bend the ends of the pipe cleaner to secure the thread spools. With scissors, trim the pipe cleaner at both ends. Set aside.

11. Cut a 2-inch piece from another straw.
12. Slide the other pipe cleaner through the straw with the ends extended.

13. Slide the third thread spool onto the straw and center it.

14. Bend the pipe cleaner to form a triangle as shown. Twist the pipe cleaner ends around each other to secure.

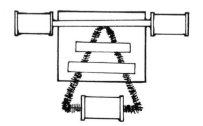

15. Attach both wheel assemblies to the bottom cardboard portion of the triangle body with masking tape. You now have mobility for the Cosmic Ray Bombarder.

58

16. To make the head, draw and cut a strip of paper 1½ inches wide by 6 inches long.

17. Fold the strip in half and open.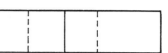

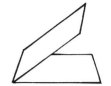

18. Measure and mark 2 inches from each end.

19. Fold these ends toward the center and open out.

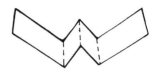

 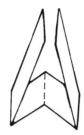

20. Fold as shown and glue upper edges together.

21. Glue the back of the head to the triangle body. The front of the head is not attached.

How I Decorated:

I cut a lightning bolt out of construction paper and glued it to a rectangular arm. I also added a special deflector shield by attaching a paper circle to the other rectangular arm. Scraps of construction paper added color and variety to the face and body. See how the eyes are a series of different-sized triangles?

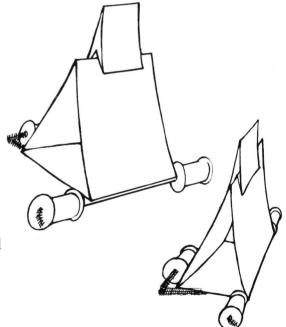

More Ideas:

Make paper antennae for your Cosmic Ray Bombarder. Add another set of arms or different kinds of arms. Use felt-tip markers to add color. Let your imagination run wild.

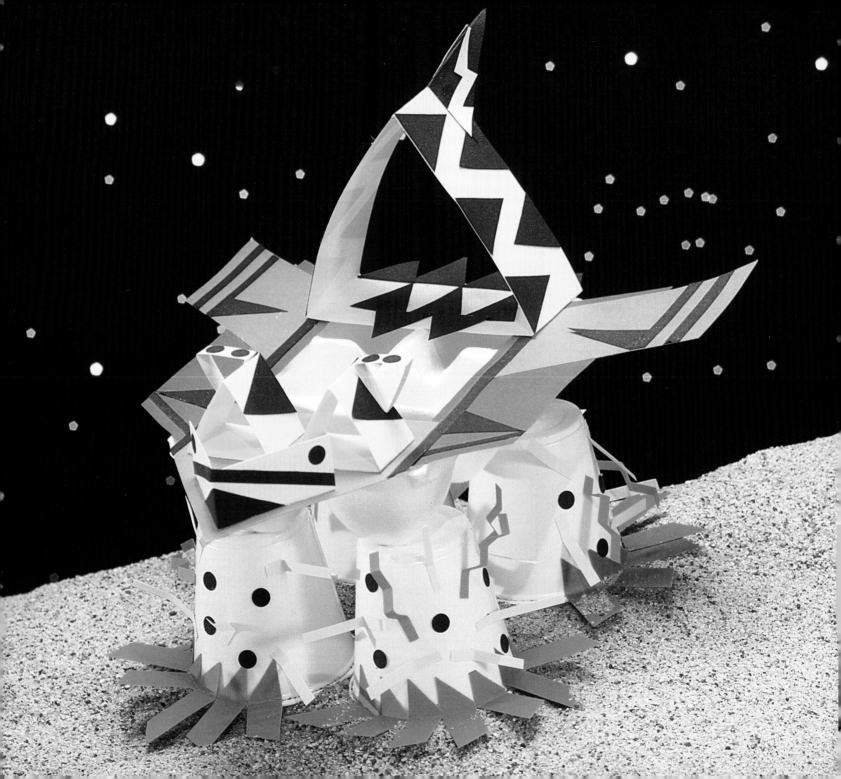

Supersonic Space Patroller

Start up the engines and get ready to blast off in the Space Patroller! Manned by the supersonic team of Bleep and Peep, the Patroller makes the heavens forever safe.

You Will Need:

colored construction paper
pencil
ruler
scissors
white liquid glue
colored felt-tip markers
1 egg carton
4 small plastic or paper cups

Let's Begin:

1. Cut the lid off the egg carton.
2. Cut the egg carton in half widthwise.

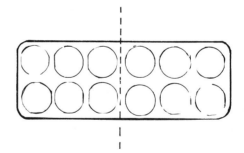

3. Glue one cup to each of the bottom corners of the carton.
4. To make the nose of the patroller, draw and cut a square of paper 4 inches wide by 4 inches long.

5. Fold the square in half and open.

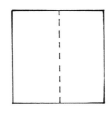

6. Cut diagonally from one corner to the fold line in the middle as shown.

7. Cut again from the other corner to the top of the fold line. You have made a triangle.

8. Glue this triangle to the front top edges of the carton body. You have made the nose piece for the patroller.

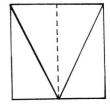

9. Draw and cut two rectangles 2 inches wide by 6 inches long.

10. Cut the corners of each rectangle to achieve a streamlined wing appearance.

11. Glue a wing to each side of the top of the carton.

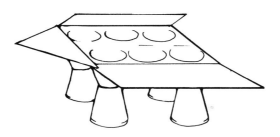

12. To make the tail of the vehicle, draw and cut a strip of paper 2 inches wide by 14 inches long.

13. Fold the strip in half and make a crease.

14. Again, fold the strip in half and make another crease.

15. Open the strip and shape it into a triangle by overlapping the two ends. Glue them together.

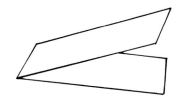

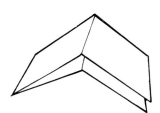
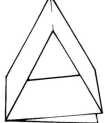

16. Glue this three-dimensional triangle to the top back end of the body.

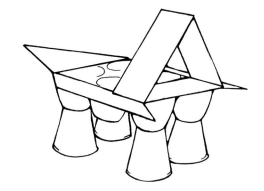

How I Decorated:

I made smaller, three-dimensional triangles by cutting narrow strips of paper and folding them twice. I opened them up, then glued the ends together. After they were dry, I glued these onto the nose piece of the patroller.

I also repeated triangle shapes on the tail and wings. I decorated the paper cups with flame shapes to give the patroller a "blast-off" feeling.

More Ideas:

Think about details you could add to make the patroller look authentic. A control panel, numbers, letters? Remember, this is supersonic, so make it look as if it will really *GO*.

Planetary Plants

Yes, plants do grow in outer space, but the atmosphere and soil cause them to develop in strange and beautiful ways. The colors and shapes of these plants can dazzle your eyes!

You Will Need:

colored construction paper
pencil
ruler
scissors
white liquid glue
poster paints and brushes
colored felt-tip markers
toilet paper tubes
You'll need one for each plant.
medium-sized kitchen bowl
A bowl 6-8 inches in diameter is fine.

Let's Begin:

1. Paint the toilet paper tube with your favorite color of poster paint. This is the trunk of your plant.

2. With a large piece of construction paper, trace a circle around the medium-sized bowl and cut it out.
3. Find the center of the circle by measuring it from edge to edge. Make a dot at the halfway point.
4. From the outer edge of the circle, make a straight cut to the center dot and stop.

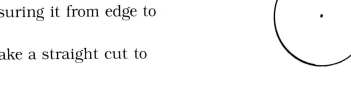

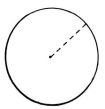

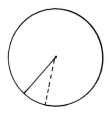

5. To form a cone from the circle, overlap the two cut edges and glue. You may need to hold this while the glue sets.
6. Place the cone over the painted tube and glue into place. You now have the base for your plant.

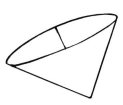

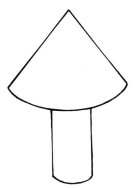

How I Decorated:

After making the basic shape of the plant, I made various-sized cones from different circle sizes by following Steps 2-5. I glued the cones in various directions. I used my imagination and made crazy shapes from simple circles, triangles, and squares cut out of contrasting colors of paper.

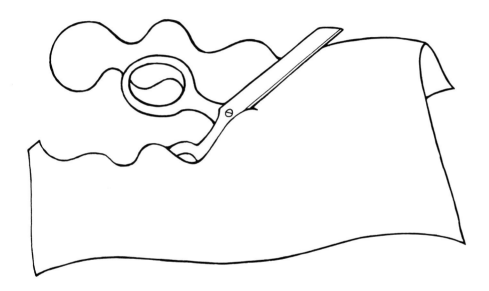

More Ideas:

Give it some thought. What other three-dimensional shapes can you use on the plants? Are there other materials you can use to decorate them? How spectacular can you make each plant?

Meteors

Of course, no star world would be complete without rocks falling from outer space. The Lunar Colony has its share of meteors scattered across the landscape.

You Will Need:

masking tape

poster paints and brushes

newspaper

wheat paste
This is wallpaper paste.

medium-sized kitchen bowl
A bowl 6-8 inches in diameter is fine.

clear acrylic spray

cardboard box

You will use the papier-mâché process to make your meteors. You can make them any size or shape and as many as you'd like. Here are the directions for making one.

Let's Begin:

1. Crumple a sheet of newspaper into a ball the approximate size and shape you want the meteor to be.

2. Tightly wrap masking tape around the newspaper ball.
3. In the bowl, mix the wheat paste according to the directions on the package.
4. Tear newspaper into strips approximately 1-2 inches wide by 6-12 inches long.

5. Dip one strip at a time into the paste. Remove excess paste with hands and apply to the newspaper-masking tape ball you made in Steps 2-3.
6. Cover the entire ball with strips, smoothing each piece carefully as you go. You can build and shape by adding more strips.
7. Allow to dry thoroughly 2-3 days.
8. Apply paints to the surface of the meteor.
9. Allow the paint to dry thoroughly.

10. Place however many meteors you have made into a large cardboard box and spray with clear acrylic spray to seal the paint surface. The cardboard box will trap any "fog" from the acrylic spray. Allow to dry.

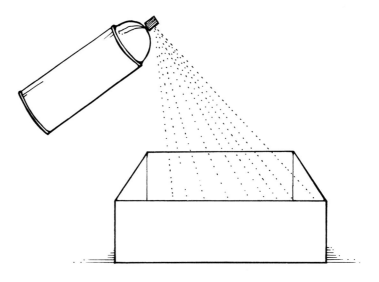

How I Decorated:

I applied different colors of paints to the meteors. I allowed the previous coat of paint to dry before applying a different color. I painted stripes and polka dots and other shapes.

More Ideas:

Create the strange planet or moon surface for your star world by filling a cardboard box with sand. Lightly press your meteors into the sand, making indentations, or "craters." The meteors will look as if they have fallen from space.